2020: A CAT ODYSSEY
"A Whimsical Journey Through a Pandemic Year"

Written by Nina Neefe
Digital Art by Tomas Hakl

www.NinasCatTales.com

Copyright @2021 Sherri Neefe
All rights reserved. No portion of this book may be reproduced—
mechanically, electronically, or by any other means, including
photocopying—without written permission from the author.
ISBNs: 978-1-7359361-3-0 (hc); 978-1-7359361-2-3 (pbk)

The *New Year* began
as it normally does

with travel and sports
and the typical buzz.

Prince Harry and Meghan
stepped back from the crown.
Australia's big fires were burning trees down.

Impeachment was big in the news every day.
Great Britain used **Brexit** for pulling away.

A basketball legend named **Kobe** was lost.
Our loved ones were hugged
and our fingers were crossed.

✓ Some highlighted events and vocabulary words are listed on back pages for learning opportunities.

Then word came from **Wuhan**
about a strange 'flu'
and cruise ships had lockdowns—
and flights canceled too.

They called it **'pandemic.'**
The world was in shock.
Then **Anthony Fauci**
became our top doc.

As **COVID-19**
soon took over our year,
we coped and we rallied
to hold what was dear.

The norm became lockdowns
and shelter-in-place
with all kinds of masks
that could cover your face.

We washed our hands often—
much more than before.
We used twenty seconds
to finish the chore.

All hand sanitizers
were quickly sold out.
TP disappeared!
What was that all about?

Some workers were heroes
with lots to endure—
essential, committed and brave,
that's for sure!

The actors stayed home,
as all filming was stopped,
and visits to movies
or hotels were dropped.

Adults worked remotely,
and kids had homeschool.
Soon virtual meetings
and learning would rule.

Our pets were so thrilled
we had more time to play.
We lived in pajamas
or soft sweats all day.

When food was delivered,
we wiped it all down.
We didn't quite know
how those germs moved around!?

Our sports were all canceled,
both local and pro.
The **Tokyo Olympics** became a 'no go.'

To be six feet apart and ensure a safe space,
they put labels and markers
all over the place.

To visit a loved one,
we kissed them through glass
and hoped that this **safeguard**
would very soon pass.

The Falcon 9 rocket launch lit up our sky.

We watched it in wonder and let out a sigh.

HAPPY BIRTHDAY

Some canceled their weddings,
while others went on.

And grads had no prom—
just a sign on the lawn!

"I DO."

The 'video greeting' was sent near and far.

We'd organize birthday parades in the car.

Our nails turned to claws,
and we all grew long hair.

At least, we had time
to clean up and repair!

For food, we'd buy curbside
and take-out to eat,
and later, we'd dine
at cafes in the street.

And who could predict
masks would have fancy styles—
new fashion accessories
hiding our smiles.

Our 'travel' was camping
and biking and hikes

and in-between that,
we had binge TV. Yikes!

NAMASTE,
MULAN.

P.E. and some workouts
were taught now online.

For some of us,
yoga outdoors was just fine.

STRETCH,
SIMON,
STRETCH!

The nose swab was now the big test of the day, as everyone tried to push worries away.

The NEOWISE comet
was gracing the Earth.

We gazed at the sky,
having faith in its worth.

The world worked together
to find a vaccine.

We prayed for an end
to our long quarantine.

Mother Nature sent warnings,
which just seemed unfair,
like fires, tornadoes,
red skies and bad air.

The Election Day Asteroid
missed us! Whoopee!
Then fall brought sad losses to mourn,
namely three.

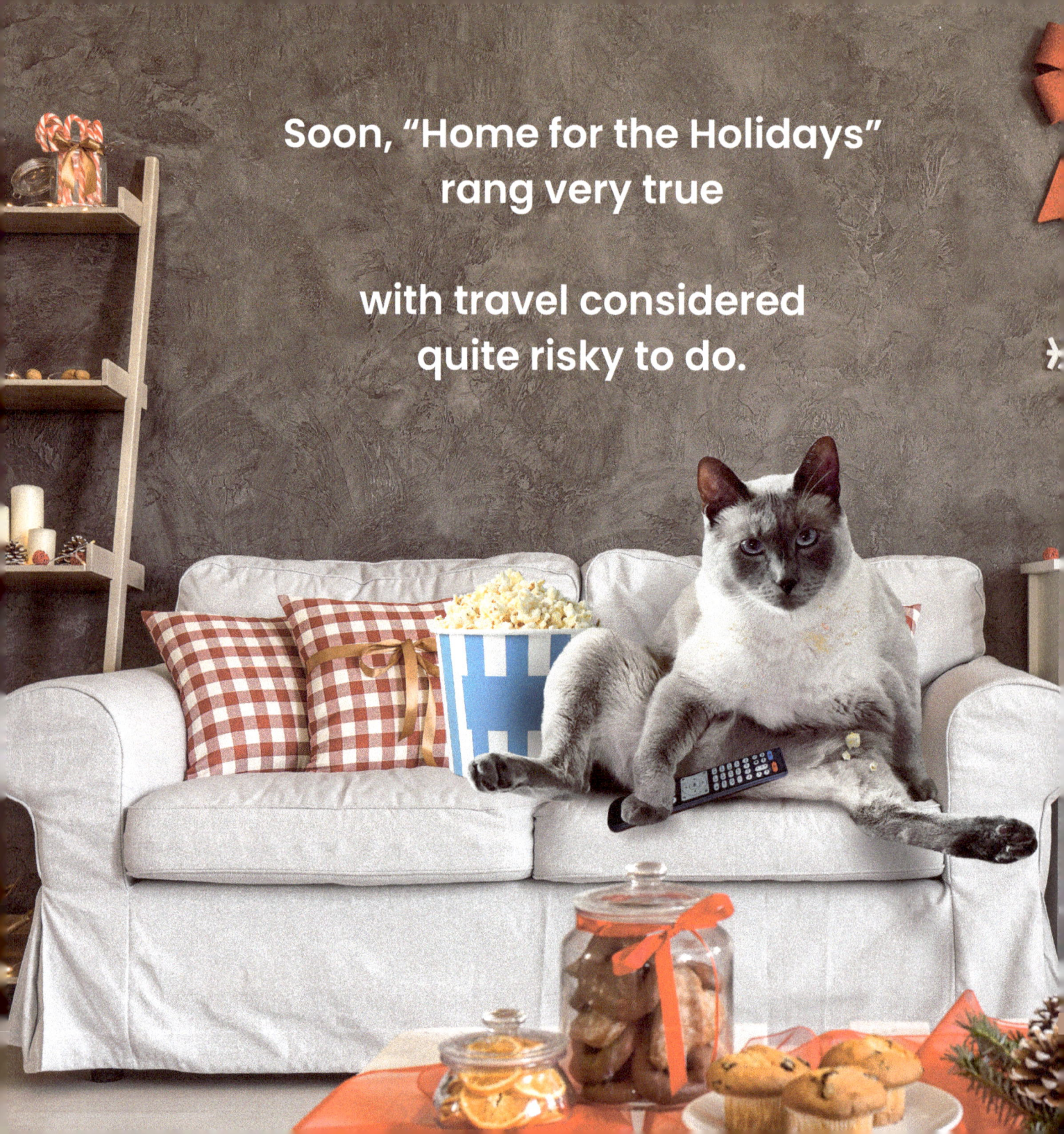

The strangest year EVER
would come to a close
with lessons and losses—
the highs and the lows.

With faith and with strength
from the Heavens above,
we've cherished our blessings
of family and love.

2020 TIMELINE OF EVENTS

Jan 1	Australia's 'Black Summer' bushfires rage for 80 days, their worst season of record.
Jan 3	Iran/US tensions flair after a US drone strike and backlash.
Jan 8	Prince Harry & Meghan officially "step back" from British senior royal duties.
Jan 10	The WHO meets to discuss a coronavirus Wuhan 'flu' outbreak.
Jan 16	US President Donald Trump is impeached, but is later acquitted on February 5th.
Jan 26	Kobe Bryant, famed Los Angeles Laker, his daughter and 7 others die in helicopter crash.
Jan 31	UK and Gibraltar formally begin Brexit, withdrawing from the European Union.
Feb 3	A cruise ship off Japan quarantines 3,700 for 4 weeks, resulting in 700 COVID cases.
Feb 20	Stock Market "Coronavirus Crash" begins, becoming the worst crash since 1929.
March 1	US begins Stay-at-Home orders; dates/terms vary (*shelter-in-place, lockdown, quarantine*).
March 11	A Pandemic is declared. NIAID Director since 1984, Dr. Anthony Fauci, gives updates.
March 24	The Olympics are postponed for first time (*they were canceled for war in 1916, 1940, 1944*).
April 20	Oil Prices plunge to lowest level in history.
May 25	George Floyd's death launches global protests and a focus on "Black Lives Matter."
May 28	Asian Giant Hornets aka "Murder Hornet" are sighted in the US.
May 30	SpaceX Falcon 9 is the first crewed spaceflight from American soil since 2011.
July 23	NEOWISE Comet C/2020 F3 comes close to earth.
August	Western Northern America fires burn millions of acres, turning skies orange.
Aug 11	Kamala Harris is first African/Asian-American woman on major presidential ticket.
Aug 13	Abraham Accords is signed for peace with Israel and UAE/United Arab Emirates.
Sept 4	Pope Benedict XVI becomes the longest-lived pope at 93 years of age.
Sept 18	Ruth Bader Ginsburg (RBG), Supreme Court Justice and trailblazer, dies at age 87.
Oct 31	Sean Connery, famously known for James Bond 007 portrayal, dies at age 90.
Nov 2	The "Election Day Asteroid" aka 2018VP1 passes close to earth.
Nov 7	Joe Biden is announced as President-Elect and 46th President of the United States.
Nov 8	Jeopardy! Host of 36 years, Alex Trebek, passes at age 80 from cancer.
Dec 8	A 90-year-old British grandmother receives the 1st non-trial dose of the COVID-19 vaccine.

GLOSSARY

COVID-19 - A highly-contagious coronavirus respiratory disease first identified in Wuhan, China, in December 2019. The International Committee on Taxonomy of Viruses (ICTV) is responsible for naming and on February 11, 2020, ICTV and the World Health Organization (WHO) announced an official name for the new disease as COVID-19. 'CO' stands for 'corona,' 'VI' for 'virus,' and 'D' for disease.

Essential - Basic, necessary; needed. "Essential Workers" during pandemic included health care, food service, and public transportation among others.

Impeachment - Action to remove public official. See timeline January 16.

Lockdown - Confinement; stay in one place.

Pandemic - A disease occurring worldwide or crossing international boundaries and usually affecting a great number of people. An epidemic is a widespread outbreak affecting a large number of people in a specific region or area. On March 11, 2020, the WHO declared the COVID-19 outbreak a pandemic.

Quarantine - Isolation to prevent spread (of a disease).

Safeguard - Something to protect or defend.

Sanitizer - A substance to kill or reduce germs.

Shelter-in-Place - Staying in a safe indoor space.

Vaccine - A preparation (usually given by injection) to help with immunity (to prevent disease). There are many COVID-19 vaccines in trials. On December 8, 2020, a COVID-19 Pfizer Vaccine was given to a 90-yr-old British Grandmother, the first person in the world to receive a vaccine outside of a trial. On December 14, 2020, a COVID-19 Vaccine Rollout began with Americans after receiving USFDA approval.

Virtual - Close to but not quite something; existing on a computer screen rather than in person.

This material is for general educational purposes, and the author assumes no responsibility for errors or omissions.

DIARY OF PERSONAL 2020 MEMORIES

AUTHOR

Nina Neefe began writing Nina's Cat Tales in early 2020 with her first children's book, *Mulan's Big Adventure*, based on the heartwarming true story of her own cat's journey to find home. Nina lives in Northern California and her love of family, her four grandchildren and her kitties inspire her to write cat-ventures. *2020: A Cat Odyssey* is Nina's third book.

DIGITAL ARTIST

This is the second book that Tomas "Tom" Hakl has helped Nina to create using his fantastical digital magic on her cats, Simon and Mulan. Tom is a photographer and digital artist from the Czech Republic and specializes in product photography, photo editing and graphic design. He enjoys the simple life and nature. And cats.

To find more of Nina's books, visit **NinasCatTales.com**

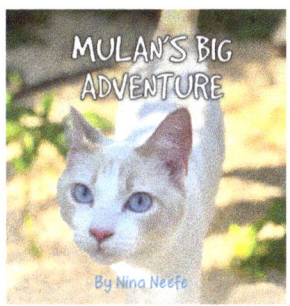
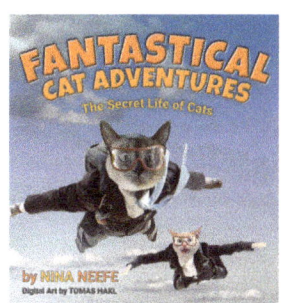

www.ingramcontent.com/pod-product-compliance
Lightning Source LLC
Chambersburg PA
CBHW051259110526
44589CB00025B/2890